THE SILK DRAGON II

Also by Arthur Sze

POETRY

The Glass Constellation: New and Collected Poems
Sight Lines
Compass Rose
The Ginkgo Light
Quipu
The Redshifting Web: Poems 1970–1998
Archipelago
River River
Dazzled
Two Ravens
The Willow Wind

TRANSLATIONS

The Silk Dragon: Translations from the Chinese

EDITOR

Chinese Writers on Writing

The Silk Dragon II

TRANSLATIONS OF CHINESE POETRY

Arthur Sze

COPPER CANYON PRESS
PORT TOWNSEND, WASHINGTON

Cover art: Chen Rong, *Nine Dragons* (detail), China, Southern Song
dynasty, dated 1244. Ink and color on paper, 18⁷⁄₁₆ × 589³⁄₁₆ in. (overall),
18³⁄₁₆ × 377⁵⁄₁₆ in. (detail), Francis Gardner Curtis Fund.
Courtesy of the Museum of Fine Arts, Boston.

Copper Canyon Press is in residence at Fort Worden State Park
in Port Townsend, Washington, under the auspices of Centrum.
Centrum is a gathering place for artists and creative thinkers from
around the world, students of all ages and backgrounds, and audi-
ences seeking extraordinary cultural enrichment.

LIBRARY OF CONGRESS CATALOGING-IN-PUBLICATION DATA
THE SILK DRAGON
Sze, Arthur.
The silk dragon: translations from the Chinese / Arthur Sze.
    p. cm.
Includes bibliographical references and index.
ISBN 1-55659-153-5 (paperback)
1. Chinese poetry — Translations into English.
i. Title: Translations of Chinese poetry. ii. Title.
PL2658.E3 S9 2000
895.1'1008—dc21
2001002044

THE SILK DRAGON II
ISBN 9781556597077 (paperback)
ISBN 9781619322950 (epub)

9 8 7 6 5 4 3 2 FIRST PRINTING

COPPER CANYON PRESS
Post Office Box 271
Port Townsend, Washington 98368
www.coppercanyonpress.org

for Micah and Sarah

Contents

Preface

The Silk Dragon II, an expanded edition of *The Silk Dragon,* includes eighteen new translations. Four are translated poems by poets who wrote in classical Chinese: Li Bai, Zhang Ji, and Wang Yuyang. Fourteen are translated poems by nine contemporary poets who wrote or write in the vernacular: Yang Mu, Chen Li, Yan Li, Yang Lian, Wang Xiaoni, Zhai Yongming, Wang Jiaxin, Xi Chuan, and Jiang Tao. The earlier edition of *The Silk Dragon* used Wade-Giles spelling, and I have retained that spelling only in the 2001 introduction, where it is rooted in time. In this new edition, I have used *pinyin* spelling throughout.

In order to convey the history of modern Chinese poetry, I need to begin with a brief background sketch about the May Fourth Movement in 1919. At the end of the First World War, when the terms of the Paris Peace Conference revealed that Western powers, instead of rewarding China for its contribution to the Allies' effort, supported Japan's claims to Shandong province, there was widespread dissent. On May 4, 1919, student representatives drew up resolutions protesting the terms of the Treaty of Versailles and calling for a mass demonstration. Defying police orders, about three thousand students protested. The May Fourth Movement grew from this demonstration at Tiananmen Square in Beijing into a national call for social, political, and cultural transformation. As part of this transformation, poets and prose writers broke from writing in classical Chinese and embraced writing in the vernacular. Although the first attempts at writing in this new language were rudimentary, the rupture was permanent. Over time, writing in the vernacular took root and grew in strength. Almost a century later, in 2007, poet and critic Xi Chuan asserted, in an essay, that the chasm that separated contemporary Chinese and classical Chinese was as large as the chasm that separated Chinese and a foreign language.

Acknowledging this break with tradition, anthologies of Chinese poetry tend to focus either on poems written in classical Chinese up to 1919 or on poems written in the vernacular after the start of the May Fourth Movement. *The Silk Dragon II* is a mini-anthology, but with its slender selection of lyrical poems that starts around 406 CE and moves chronologically into our current time, I hope this collection, by bringing classical and vernacular poetry together within the same volume, provides a unique entry into the rich tradition of Chinese poetry. And, as I said in my 2001 introduction, "where I have chosen a single poem by a poet, it is in no way an indication that the poet merits only one poem in this anthology; it is merely that I have only been able to make one translation with which I am satisfied."

The primary focus to the first edition of *The Silk Dragon* was on poetry written in classical Chinese. That anthology started with Tao Qian (365–427) whose "fields and gardens" poetry was imbued with contemplative insight. The major Tang-dynasty poets, Wang Wei, Li Bai, Du Fu, and Li Shangyin, were among those highlighted. I then moved beyond the Tang and included poems from other eras that extend the lineage and scope of lyrical Chinese poetry. From the Song dynasty I translated poems by Su Dongpo and Li Qingzhao; from the Yuan dynasty, poems by Ma Zhiyuan; from the Ming and Qing dynasties, poems by Shen Zhou and Bada Shanren.

In presenting the classical Chinese poems, I want to convey that this tradition and the evolution of this poetry are neither homogeneous nor linear. For one thing, poets from different eras used many different forms. In the Tang dynasty, a majority of poets wrote in the *shi* form, where there are usually five characters to a line with one prescribed caesura, 1-2 / 3-4-5, or seven characters to a line with two caesuras, 1-2 / 3-4 / 5-6-7. The poems were traditionally chanted, and *shi* poems draw emotional resonance from the silences as well as the sounds. Wang Wei excelled in the *jueju,* or quatrain form, which employed five or seven characters to a line and was only four lines long. Du Fu excelled in the *lushi,* or regulated verse, a poem in eight lines of five or seven characters, with requirements for parallelism in the two middle couplets. This form also had complex requirements for tonal contrast.

Toward the end of the Tang dynasty (618–906), a new lyric form, *ci,* emerged. The *ci* forms were based on popular songs, and the titles to *ci* poems referred to melodies on which the poems were composed. In the Song dynasty (960–1279), Li Qingzhao excelled in this form, and the titles to her poems, such as "To the Tune of 'Intoxicated in the Shadows of Flowers,'" indicate the specific song and melody at hand. In the Yuan dynasty (1280–1368), the ruling Mongols promoted opera, and a new form of opera song, *xiqu,* emerged. Other songs, *sanqu,* independent of operas, began to be written. Short and highly compressed, these songs utilized lines of unequal length. Ma Zhiyuan, a leading playwright, wrote in the *qu* form, and his poems translated here also show their connection to music with such titles as "To the Tune of 'Sky-Clear Sand': Autumn Thoughts."

Consciously exploring the Chinese poetic tradition, I decided to expand the range by including a poem by the renowned painter Shen Zhou. And to extend the connection between poetry and painting, I selected poems by the great painter Bada Shanren. Bada Shanren frequently inscribed Chan-imbued poems on his paintings, and though these poems were never included in traditional anthologies of Chinese poetry, I believe his poems are highly original and deserve a place in the canon. To further extend the connection between poetry and painting, I have newly translated four poems by Li Bai, Zhang Ji, and Wang Yuyang that are all painterly in their effects.

Over the centuries, despite the enormous ruptures and transformations in the forms of classical Chinese poetry, demarcated by changes in dynastic leadership, there is also continuity. Poets up until 1919 continued to write in the *shi* as well as other forms. The rupture created by the May Fourth Movement, when writers replaced classical language with the vernacular, was more complete than the ruptures that preceded it. A pivotal poet was Wen Yiduo, who knew the classical tradition intimately but who chose to subvert and transform it. Wen Yiduo's poems are memorable for their immediacy, their architectural rigor, and their rhythmical innovation.

In 2001, I ended *The Silk Dragon* with four poems by Yan Zhen, a farmer-poet who lived on a commune in Sichuan province during the 1950s. At their best, these poems have a folk quality that, arguably, shows roots going as far back as the first anthology of Chinese poetry, the *Shijing*. At their worst, these are socialist-realist poems that portray a stereotypical image of ameliorating social conditions in commune life. As such, they epitomize the kind of poetry promoted through the 1950s and '60s. This ending to the 2001 edition of *The Silk Dragon* has always felt incomplete.

In the years following the publication of *The Silk Dragon,* as I continued to extend and deepen my understanding of Chinese poetry, I turned to the contemporary. To what extent were poets in China furthering a rupture with the past? To what extent were Chinese poets drawing on Western poetry as their primary source of inspiration? To what extent were poets drawing on classical Chinese poetry but not being bound by it? These are the questions that motivated me, and they turned out to have no simple answer. Certainly, contemporary Chinese poets have drawn immense inspiration from Russian and then Western poetry in translation. And another great historical rupture, the Cultural Revolution, has to be considered as well.

During the Cultural Revolution (1966–76), all the universities were closed. Students were organized into groups of Red Guards, and intellectuals were targeted across the country as counterrevolutionaries. Millions of people were tortured and executed. The poetry of that time was heavily socialist-realist, but when Mao Zedong died and that tragic period ended, a young generation of "Misty" poets emerged. The term *misty poet* was originally a pejorative one, coined by the literary establishment who felt that, after years of clear socialist-realist poetry, poets were writing a highly personal, idiosyncratic poetry whose meaning was hard to pin down. The Misty poets by no means wrote a unified kind of poetry, nor did the waves of poets who came after. As I looked at contemporary Chinese poetry, I was not interested in what school or group a poet might or might not belong to; instead, I wanted poems that stood out for their imaginative language and singular power. Over time I've chosen poems by poets who write in Chinese, in a wide variety of styles, and who, at this moment, live in China, Taiwan, Germany, and the United States.

As I embarked on these new translations of contemporary Chinese poetry, I was fortunate to meet almost all the poets I translated, at different times, at different international poetry festivals. In 2002, I went to Taiwan and met Yang Mu and Chen Li. I immediately admired Chen Li's poems and selected two to translate. Many years later, Michelle Yeh was assembling a collection of Yang Mu's poetry in English translation, and she offered me rough drafts of a few poems. I have included two, and, because the drafts were substantive, I have listed our names as cotranslators.

In 2007, at the Pamirs Poetry Journey at Huangshan in China, I met Yang Lian, Wang Xiaoni, Xi Chuan, and Yan Li. As part of that festival, I translated two poems by Yang Lian. A year later, Arts Council England helped to arrange the Yellow Mountain Poetry Festival in the United Kingdom. Before that festival, all the poets met at Atlantic College in Wales, and there was an intensive translation session where poets translated each other's works. During this time, I translated a poem by Xi Chuan and another by Yan Li. In 2013, I attended the Rainbow Bridge Poets Gathering at the Slender West Lake; as part of that festival, I met Jiang Tao and Zhai Yongming and translated one of Jiang Tao's poems. At each of these poetry festivals, I had the opportunity to work on drafts while the poets were present, and they responded to questions when I had them. In 2022, I had the pleasure of meeting Wang Jiaxin in New York City. He showed me three poems; I was excited by them and decided to translate them into English as well.

In looking at the group of contemporary Chinese poets I initially translated, I realized that organizers of the poetry festivals always paired me with other male poets. Although I had met Wang Xiaoni and Zhai Yongming, I didn't have the opportunity to translate any of their poetry; because they are exceptional poets, I decided to translate a poem by each of them to include here. I did not have the benefit of asking them questions as I worked on the translations, but my aunt, Pan Jiaxiu, provided assistance. I also thank George O'Connell and Diana Shi for checking my translation drafts with a character-by-character reading of those two poems. And, finally, I thank Michelle Yeh and my wife, Carol Moldaw, for reviewing the entire manuscript.

There are of course classical as well as contemporary poets I would have liked to include—Bei Dao and Duo Duo, among contemporary poets, though they are well represented by other translators.

I hope the movement from Tao Qian through the Tang poets and extending through Li Qingzhao, Ma Zhiyuan, and Wen Yiduo offers an experience of the many kinds of poetry that all belong to the lineage and evolution of Chinese poetry. I'm interested in continuity and growth as well as rupture. I believe it is illuminating, for instance, to read Li Bai's "Night Thoughts" and then jump over a thousand years ahead to read Wang Xiaoni's "Very White Moonlight" and consider the relationship. One can read Yang Lian's "Memorial to a Tree at the Street Corner," then go back over a thousand years and read the Tang poems included here and consider the implications of "the Tang dynasty like a lantern suddenly switched on." And one can admire the classical beauty of Liu Zongyuan's "Snow on the River," then contrast it to the troubling psychological insight in Wang Jiaxin's "Ice Anglers." The poems are in conversation with each other, and, for Chinese poetry, an expanding web may be a more appropriate image than a line, or lines, of development. I hope readers come to a better understanding and appreciation of the vitality, diversity, and power of the Chinese poetic tradition and how it continues to flourish today. And in the end, I hope these translations move as poems.

THE SILK DRAGON II

Introduction to *The Silk Dragon* (2001)

The translation of Chinese poems into English has always been a source of inspiration for my own evolution as a poet. In 1971, as a student at the University of California at Berkeley, I majored in poetry. Also studying Chinese language and literature, I became interested in translating the great T'ang-dynasty poets—Li Po, Tu Fu, Wang Wei, among others—because I felt I could learn from them. I felt that by struggling with many of the great poems in the Chinese literary tradition, I could best develop my voice as a poet. Years later, in 1983, after publishing *Dazzled,* my third book of poetry, I translated a new group of Chinese poems, again feeling that it would help me discern greater possibilities for my own writing. I was drawn to the clarity of T'ao Ch'ien's lines, to the subtlety of Ma Chih-yüan's lyrics, and to Wen I-to's sustained, emotional power. In 1996, after completing my book *Archipelago,* I felt the need to translate yet another group of Chinese poems: I was particularly drawn to the Ch'an-influenced work of Pa-ta-shan-jen and to the extremely condensed and challenging, transformational poems of Li Ho and Li Shang-yin.

I know translation is an "impossible" task, and I have never forgotten the Italian phrase *traduttori/traditori:* "translators/traitors." Which translation does not in some way betray its original? In considering the process of my own translations, I am aware of loss and transformation, of destruction and renewal. Since I first started to write poetry, I have only translated poems that have deeply engaged me; and it has sometimes taken me many years to feel ready to work on one. I remember that in 1972 I read Li

Shang-yin's untitled poems and felt baffled by them; now, more than twenty-five years later, his verses—veiled, mysterious, and full of longing—strike me as some of the great love poems in classical Chinese.

To show how I create a translation in English, I am going to share stages and drafts of a translation from one of Li Shang-yin's untitled poems. I like to begin by writing the Chinese characters out on paper. I know that my own writing of Chinese is awkward and rudimentary, but by writing out the characters in their particular stroke order, I can begin to sense the inner motion of the poem in a way that I cannot by just reading the characters on the page. Once I've written out the characters, I look up each in Robert H. Mathews's *Chinese-English Dictionary* and write down the sound and tone along with a word, phrase, or cluster that helps mark its field of energy and meaning. I go through the entire poem doing this groundwork. After I have created this initial cluster of words, I go back through and, because a Chinese character can mean so many different things depending on its context, I remove words or phrases that appear to be inappropriate and keep those that appear to be relevant. In the case of Li Shang-yin's untitled poem, I now have a draft that looks like the figure on the facing page.

In looking at this regulated eight-line poem, I know that each of its seven-character lines has two predetermined caesuras, so that the motion in Chinese is 1-2 / 3-4 / 5-6-7. I try to catch the tonal flow and sense the silences. I know that the tones from Mathews's dictionary only give me the barest approximation. T'ang-dynasty poems are most alive when they are chanted. The sounds are very different from the Mandarin dialect that I speak. Yet I can, for instance, guess that the sound of *tuan⁴*, the first character in line six, is sharp and emphatic. I also feel that characters three and four in line six—*hsiao¹* and *hsi²*—have

鳳	尾	香	羅	薄	幾	重
male phoenix	*tail/s*	*fragrant*	*gauze, thin silk*	*thin, slight*	*how many*	*layers, folds*
feng⁴	wei³	hsiang¹	lo²	po²	chi³	ch'ung²
碧	文	圓	頂	夜	深	逢
green jade	*elegant, refined*	*round*	*the top*	*night*	*deep*	*meet with*
pi⁴	wen²	yüan²	ting³	yeh⁴	shen¹	feng²
扇	裁	月	魄	羞	難	掩
fan	*to cut*	*moon*	*form, shape*	*shame, blush*	*difficult*	*conceal*
shan⁴	ts'ai²	yüeh⁴	p'o⁴	hsiu¹	nan²	yen³
車	走	雷	聲	語	未	通
carriage	*departs*	*thunder*	*sound/s*	*word/s*	*not yet*	*get through*
ch'e¹	tsou³	lei²	sheng¹	yü³	wei⁴	t'ung¹
曾	是	寂	寥	金	燼	暗
once, already	*is*	*silent*	*empty*	*gold*	*ashes, embers*	*dark, cloudy*
ts'eng²	shih⁴	chi⁴	liao²	chin¹	chin⁴	an⁴
斷	無	消	息	石	榴	紅
cut off	*no, without*	*—ebb and flow—*		*—pomegranate—*		*red*
tuan⁴	wu²	hsiao¹	hsi²	shih²	liu²	hung²
班	騅	只	繫	垂	楊	柳
mottled	*piebald horse*	*only, but*	*tie, bind*	*hang down*	*—willow—*	
pan¹	chui¹	chih³	hsi⁴	ch'ui²	yang²	liu³
何	處	西	南	任	好	風
what, which	*place*	*—southwest—*		*allow, confide in*	*good*	*wind*
ho²	ch'u⁴	hsi¹	nan²	jen⁴	hao³	feng¹

an onomatopoetic quality to suggest ebb and flow. In double-checking this phrase in the dictionary, I realize it has the primary meaning of "news and information"; there is no news, and the speaker is in a state of heightened isolation. In looking at the visual configuration of the characters, I am again struck by the first character in line six, *tuan*[4]. Here the character contains the image of scissors cutting silk, and I wonder if this can be extended to develop an insight into the poem.

I proceed by writing a rough draft in English: trying to write eight lines in English that are equivalent to the eight lines in Chinese. I realize immediately that the translation is too cramped. I look back at the Chinese and decide to use *two* lines in English for each line of Chinese. I also decide to emphasize the second caesura of each line in Chinese so that in English there's a line break after the meaning of the fourth character in each line of the Chinese original.

I write out another draft in which sixteen lines in English now stand for the eight lines in Chinese. All the lines in English are flush left, but the blocklike form does not do justice to the obliquely cutting motion of the poem. To open it up and clarify the architecture, I decide to indent all of the even-numbered lines. I go through another series of drafts, oftentimes incorporating English words that I've listed on the page with Chinese characters, though I don't feel compelled to use all of them. At this transitional stage, I have something that looks like the following version (prior to the deletions and additions):

> phoenix tails, fragrant silk,
>
> ⌐ *folds*
> how many thin ~~layers~~.
> under the ~~elegant~~ green round canopy

↳ opens to

she ~~encounters~~ the deep night.

the fan cuts the moon's shape

┌ but　　　　　*┌ blush*
↓　　　　　　　*↓*

~~and~~ can't conceal her ~~shame~~.

a carriage goes, thunder sounds,

┌ didn't
↓

the words ~~can't~~ get through.

a while in the desolate quiet
×̳=̳=̳=̳=̳

gold embers in the dark.

nothing now but　　　　*┌ the ebb and flow of*
　　　　　　　　　　　↓
↳ ~~cut off, no word, who could be pouring~~

~~a measure of~~ red pomegranate wine?

a piebald horse is yet tied

┌ dangling
↓

to a ~~trailing~~ willow.

┌from
↓

×̳ ̳a̳n̳d̳ ̳w̳h̳e̳r̳e̳ ̳i̳s̳ ̳t̳h̳e̳ ̳p̳l̳a̳c̳e̳ ~~in~~ the southwest

where the fine breeze can blow?

At this point, if there are books of Chinese translations that I think might be helpful, I look at them to see whether they have commentaries that are relevant. In François Cheng's *Chinese Poetic Writing* I find that lines one and two "describe the bedcurtain of a bridal chamber," that "to pluck a willow branch" means to visit a courtesan, that red pomegranate wine might be served at a wedding feast and connotes explosive desire, and that the southwest breeze alludes to a phrase by Ts'ao Chih (192–232), "I would become that southwest wind / waft all the way to your bosom." I find these comments insightful but do not want to incorporate them overtly into my translation. Because Li Shang-yin's great strength is his oblique exactitude, I want my translation to hint at these elements.

I now look at my very rough translation and go back to the original Chinese. My experience of the poem is that a solitary woman is lamenting the absence of her lover and longs for him even as she worries that he is unfaithful. I go back through my translation, cross out certain phrases, and substitute new phrases wherever they seem better. With the second line, I decide that it is more appropriate to have the silk in folds than in layers. In line three, the phrase "elegant green round canopy" is cumbersome; I decide the word "elegant" is too stated and should be removed. It's so hard in a contemporary poem to use an adjective like "elegant" and not cause a boomerang effect. I read on and decide that "encounters" is too neutral. To make the longing more overt, I change it to "opens to the deep night." In line six, I change "and" to "but," and substitute "blush" for "shame." I'm happy with this last change: the "blush" will help foreshadow the "red pomegranate wine" and also suggests the red of desire. In line eight, I change "can't" to "didn't," though I'm not sure this is better. In line nine, I mark with an x and double-underline the word "desolate." This word is another loaded adjective, but nothing comes to mind as a good replacement, so I mark it with an x to tell myself to come back to it. I am totally dissatisfied with line eleven and strike it out. I go back to the page with characters and reincorporate "ebb and flow." With line fourteen, I am uneasy about "trailing" and insert "dangling." Line fifteen strikes me as too wordy, but again nothing comes to mind, so I mark it with an x and a double-underline.

At this point, I put the translation away for a few weeks. I brood on it, and if some changes come to mind, jot them down on the side. But I usually wait until I feel I can revise with intensity and clarity. When I finally sit down and rework the translation, I decide that "the deep quiet" opens up the emotional space in a way that "the desolate quiet" can't. I decide to foreground the gold embers and make them a more active presence; the verb "scintillate" leaps into my mind. To suggest that red pomegranate wine connotes explosive desire, and to make the configuration of sounds more alive, I replace the static "a measure of red pomegranate wine" with the active "pulsing red pomegranate wine." I also decide to break the symmetry of the indented lines by further indenting the very last line; I think this heightens the cutting effect of the ending. You can see these significant changes incorporated into the final version:

UNTITLED (II) *by Li Shang-yin*

Phoenix tails, fragrant silk,
    so many thin folds.
Under the round green canopy,
    she opens herself to the night.
A fan cuts the moon's shape
    but can't conceal her blush.
The carriage goes, thunder sounds;
    the words couldn't get through.
A while in the deep quiet,
    gold embers scintillate:
nothing now but the ebb and flow of
    pulsing red pomegranate wine.
A piebald horse is yet tied
    to a dangling willow.
And where out of the southwest
      can the fine breeze blow?

I hope going through this poem at length shows how arduous but also how rewarding translation can be. *The Silk Dragon* presents in English the work of eighteen poets in chronological order, beginning with T'ao Ch'ien (365–427) and ending with Yen Chen, who published in the 1950s. It is a collection of personal favorites; yet, slim as it is, I hope it presents a complex vision of the vitality, diversity, and power of the Chinese poetic tradition.

Many American readers are by now familiar with Li Po, Wang Wei, and Tu Fu, but too few readers know Li Ho, Li Shang-yin, Ma Chih-yüan, Shen Chou, Pa-ta-shan-jen, Wen I-to, or Yen Chen. There exists a huge gulf in many readers' awareness between the early T'ang poets and the contemporary Misty School poets. There is no way a small volume such as this can fill in those gaps, but I want to single out poems of particular excellence that can serve as landmarks. And where I have chosen a single poem by a poet, it is in no way an indication that the poet merits only one poem in this anthology; it is merely that I have only been able to make one translation with which I am satisfied.

This collection assembles all the translations I consider finished; because there is a poet who lived as early as 400 CE, and because I have relied so heavily on Mathews's *Chinese-English Dictionary*, I have used the Wade-Giles romanization system.

There are several people I want to thank for help with these translations. In 1971, Ts'ai Mei-hsi taught conversational Mandarin at the University of California at Berkeley; I was in one of his classes, and he generously agreed to help me review poems by Li Po, Tu Fu, and Wang Wei, and also introduced me to Yen Chen's work. In 1983, Pan Chia-hsiu helped me with the T'ao Ch'ien, Li Ch'ing-chao, Ma Chih-yüan, and Wen I-to. In recent years, Xue Di helped me with a poem by Li Ho, and Yang Hsiao-hui helped me with another by Li Shang-yin. Because many of the Li Ho and

Li Shang-yin poems have difficult allusions, I have appended notes at the end of the book to clarify them.

In closing, I want to mention my idea that the mind is a dragon. In Chinese culture, a dragon embodies magic, transformation, and energy. Wolfram Eberhard once wrote, "As a magic animal, the dragon is able to shrink to the size of a silkworm; and then it can swell up till it fills the space between heaven and earth." Li Shang-yin wrote in a famous untitled poem, included in this collection, "A spring silkworm spins silk / up to the instant of death." That phrase can be taken as a metaphor for how a poet works with language. "The silk dragon," then, is my metaphor for poetry.

ARTHUR SZE, 2001

TAO QIAN

Drinking Wine (I)

A green pine is in the east garden,
but the many grasses obscure it.
A frost wipes out all the other species,
and then I see its magnificent tall branches.
In a forest, men do not notice it,
but standing alone, it is a miracle.
I hang a jug of wine on a cold branch;
then stand back, and look again and again.
My life spins with dreams and illusions.
Why then be fastened to the world?

TAO QIAN

Drinking Wine (II)

I built my house near where others live,
and yet without noise of horse or carriage.
You ask, how can this be?
A distant mind leaves the earth around it.
I pick chrysanthemums below the eastern fence,
then gaze at mountains to the south.
The mountain air is fine at sunset;
flying birds go back in flocks.
In this there is a truth—
I wish to tell you, but lose the words.

TAO QIAN

Drinking Wine (III)

Fall chrysanthemums have fine colors.
I pluck a few blossoms speckled with dew
and float one in wine to forget my sorrow
and leave the world far behind.
Alone, I pour myself a cup, but when
it's empty, the jug tips and refills it.
At dusk, all movement slows to a stop.
The birds fly to the woods, singing.
I whistle and whistle on the east veranda—
go ahead, embrace this life!

TAO QIAN

Returning to Fields and Gardens (I)

When I was young, I did not fit in
with others, and simply loved the hills and mountains.
By mistake, I fell into the dusty net,
and before I knew it, it was thirty years!
The caged bird longs for the old forest.
The fish in the pond misses the old depths.
I cultivate land along the southern wilds,
and, keeping to simplicity, return to fields and garden.
Ten acres now surround my house;
it is thatched, and has eight, nine rooms.
Elms and willows shade the back eaves.
Peach and plum trees are lined out the front hall.
The distant village is hazy, hazy: and
slender, slender, the smoke hanging over houses.
Dogs bark in the deep lane, and a rooster
crows on top of a mulberry tree.
My house untouched by the dust of the world—
ample leisure in these bare rooms.
I was held so long inside a narrow bird-
cage, but now, at last, can return to nature.

TAO QIAN

Returning to Fields and Gardens (II)

I plant beans below the southern hill;
there grasses flourish and bean sprouts are sparse.
At dawn, I get up, clear out a growth of weeds,
then go back, leading the moon, a hoe over my shoulder.

Now the path is narrow, grasses and bushes are high.
Evening dew moistens my clothes;
but so what if my clothes are wet—
I choose not to avoid anything that comes.

WANG HAN

Song of Liangzhou

The grape wine is beautiful
as light shines into the cup at night.
I would like to drink
but the lute urges me to mount my horse.
Sir, if I am lying drunk on the battlefield,
please do not laugh.
Since ancient times,
how many soldiers ever returned?

WANG WEI

Bamboo Grove

I sit alone in the secluded bamboo grove
and play the zither and whistle along.
In the deep forest no one knows,
the bright moon comes to shine on me.

WANG WEI

Deer Park

The mountain is empty, no man can be seen;
but the echo of human sounds is heard.
Returning sunlight, entering the deep forest,
shines again on green moss, above.

WANG WEI

Xinyi Village

At the tips of branches,
       hibiscus
opening red calyxes
       deep in the mountains.
A stream, hut:
       yet no one.
The flowers bloom
       and fall, bloom and fall.

from "Miscellaneous Poems"

Sir, you come from my native home
and should know the affairs there.
The day you left, beside the silk-paned window—
did the cold plum sprout flowers or not?

WANG WEI

Highland

Peach blossom's red, filled with night rain.
The willow, green,
is still veiled in the mist of spring.
The boy has not swept up the fallen petals.
Orioles singing,
the mountain hermit is yet sleeping.

WANG WEI

Sending Off Mr. Yuan

The rain settles a light dust in Wei City.
Green, green are the willows by the traveler's hut.
Sir, I advise you to empty another cup of wine,
for west of Yang Pass you will meet no friend.

LI BAI

Drinking Alone with the Moon

Among the flowers with a jug of wine,
I pour, alone, lacking companions,
and, raising cup, invite the bright moon:
facing my shadow makes three people.
But the moon is unable to drink,
and my shadow just follows my body;
for a time, the moon leads the shadow—
be joyous as long as it's spring!
I sing, and the moon wavers.
I dance, and the shadow stumbles.
When sober, we were intimate friends;
now drunk, each of us separates.
May we be bound and travel without anxieties—
may we meet in the far Milky Way.

Song of Zhanggan

When my hair just began to cover my forehead,
I was plucking flowers, playing in front of the gate.
You came along riding a bamboo stick horse,
circling and throwing green plums.
Together we lived in Zhanggan Village
never suspicious of our love.
At fourteen, I became your wife,
my shy face never opened.
I lowered my head, faced the dark wall,
to your thousand calls, never a response.
At fifteen, I became enlightened,
was willing to be dust with you, ashes with you.
Always preserving you in my heart,
why should I ascend the terrace to look for your return?
At sixteen, you traveled far, through
Qutang Gorge, by rocks and swirling waters . . .
And in the fifth month, they are impassable,
monkeys wailing to the sky . . .
By our door where you left footprints,
mosses, one by one, grew over;
too deep to be swept away!
Leaves fall early in the autumn wind.

In lunar August, yellow butterflies
hovered in pairs over the west garden grasses.
My heart hurt at this sight, beauty flickering . . .
Sooner or later, if you return through the Three Ba district,
send home first. I will meet you,
ignore the long distance, even to Long Wind Sands.

LI BAI

Night Thoughts

The moonlight falls by my bed.
I wonder if there's frost on the ground.
I raise my head to look at the moon,
then ease down, thinking of home.

LI BAI

Question and Answer in the Green Mountains

You ask me why I live in the green mountains;
I laugh and don't answer—I'm at peace.
Peach blossoms on flowing water go into the distance.
There is another sky and earth not among men.

LI BAI

Sitting Alone with Jingting Mountain

All the birds fly high and vanish.
A lone cloud drifts by.
Never tiring of gazing at each other—
now, only Jingting Mountain.

LI BAI

The Lotus

Lotus flowers blossomed, and the river was drenched in red.
Sir, you said the lotuses were more beautiful than me.
Yesterday, when I passed by the flowers,
why, then, didn't people look at the lotus?

LI BAI

To the Tune of "Clear Happiness"

Clouds remind me of her dress
and flowers of her face.
The spring wind caresses the rail
where dew clusters
on the blossoms.
If you do not see her majesty
on the top of Jade Mountain,
perhaps you will meet her
(as the moon sinks)
on the Green Jasper Terrace.

Return to Qiang Village

Shaggy red clouds in the west—
the sun's foot is down to level earth.
By the wicker gate, sparrows are chirping.
The traveler returns from over a thousand *li*.

Wife and children panic at my presence;
quieted, they still wipe tears.
In this age of turmoil, I floated and meandered.
A miracle of chance to return alive!

Neighbors crowd the fence tops
and also sigh and sob.
In the deep night, we are again holding candles,
facing each other as in a dream.

DU FU

Spring View

The nation is broken, but hills and rivers remain.
Spring is in the city, grasses and trees are thick.
Touched by the hard times, flowers shed tears.
Grieved by separations, birds are startled in their hearts.

The beacon fires burned for three consecutive months.
A letter from home would be worth ten thousand pieces of gold.
As I scratch my white head, the hairs become fewer:
so scarce that I try in vain to fasten them with a pin.

DU FU

Night at the Tower

At year's end, yin and yang
        hasten the shortening daylight.
Frost and snow at the sky's edge
        clear into a crisp, cold night.
At fifth watch, drums and bugles
        sound a piercing grief,
while over Three Gorges, shadows
        of the Milky Way sway and rock.
In the countryside, wild sobs
        resounded through homes after the destruction.
Here and there, tribal songs
        of fishermen and woodcutters arise.
Lying-Dragon and Leaping-Horse
        have disintegrated into yellow dust;
let the news of all our affairs
        . . . be still and hushed.

Moonlight Night

This evening in Fuzhou my wife
can only look out alone at the moon.
From Changan I pity my children
who cannot yet remember or understand.

Her hair is damp in the fragrant mist.
Her arms are cold in the clear light.
When will we lean beside the window
and the moon shine on our dried tears?

DU FU

Thoughts on a Night Journey

A slight wind stirs the grass along the bank.
A lone boat sails with a mast in the night.
The stars are pulled down to the vast plain,
and the moon bobs in the river's flow.

My name couldn't ever be famous in literature:
I have resigned office from sickness and age.
Drifting and drifting, what am I
but a solitary gull between earth and heaven?

ZHANG JI

Mooring at Night by the Maple Bridge

Moon sinks,
    crows cry:
        a frost-full sky.

River maples,
    fishing fires—
        grieving in sleep.

At Gusu,
    beyond the city walls:
        Cold Mountain Temple.

Midnight,
    a bell sounds—
        reaching a traveler's boat.

BAI JUYI

A Question Addressed to Mr. Liu

I have some newly brewed "green ant" wine
and a small stove made of red clay.
As evening comes, the sky threatens snow:
could we not drink a cup?

Snow on the River

Over thousands of mountains
birds no longer fly.
Over ten thousand paths
no more trace of humans.
On a lone boat, an old man
in a bamboo hat and palm coat,
alone fishing,
in the cold snowy river.

LI HE

Flying Light

Flying light, flying light—
I urge you to drink a cup of wine.
I do not know the height of blue heaven
nor the extent of yellow earth.
I only sense the moon's cold,
sun's burn sear us.
Eat bear, and you'll grow fat;
eat frog, and you'll waste away.
Where is the Spirit Lady?
And where the Great Unity?
East of the sky is the Ruo tree:
underneath, a dragon, torch in mouth.
I will cut off the dragon's feet
and chew the dragon's flesh:
then morning will never return
and evening cannot bend.
Old men will not die
nor young men weep.
Why then swallow yellow gold
or gulp down white jade?
Who is Ren Hungzi
riding a white ass through the clouds?

Liu Che, in Maoling tomb, is just a heap of bones.
And Ying Zheng rots in his catalpa coffin,
wasting all that abalone.

Song of the Collator's Sword in the Spring Bureau

Elder, inside your casket
           is three feet of water.
This sword once plunged
           into Wu Lake and beheaded a dragon.
A slash of brightest moonlight
           shaves the cold dew.
A white satin sash lies flat
           and will not ruffle in wind.
The hilt of ancient shark-womb skin
           has bristling caltrops.
A white-breasted seabird
           tempered into a white pheasant's tail.
Truly this is a sliver
           of Jing Ge's heart!
Do not let it shine on
           the characters in the Spring Bureau.
Twisted strands of coiling gold
           hang from the hilt.
The sword's brilliant shine
           can sunder an Indigo Field jade.
Draw, and the White King
           of the West will quake—
wailing and wailing, his demon
           mother in the autumn wilds.

LI HE

Autumn Comes

Wind in the plane tree startles the heart: a grown man's grief.
By dying lamplight, crickets are weeping cold threads.
Who will ever read the green bamboo slips of this book?
Or stop the ornate worms from gnawing powdery holes?
Such thoughts tonight must disentangle in my gut.
In the humming rain, a fragrant spirit consoles this poet.
On an autumn grave, a ghost chants Bao Zhao's poem,
and his spiteful blood, buried a thousand years, is now green jade.

DU MU

Anchored at Qinhuai River

Mist veils the cold water,
and moonlight veils the sands.
I anchored at Qinhuai
near the wine taverns.
Women singers, not knowing
the agonies of a destroyed nation,
still sing the tune of
"Back Court Flowers" on the farther bank.

DU MU

Easing My Heart

Ill-fated, I carried wine
while traveling through the world.
Zhao Feiyan's waist was so slender and delicate:
she was weightless in my arms.
For ten years I indulged;
now, in Yangzhou, awaken from my dream:
having gained in the blue houses
only a drifting name.

The Brocade Zither

This brocade zither, for no apparent reason, has fifty strings.

Each string and each bridge bring to mind a blossoming year.

Zhuangzi had a morning dream of a confused butterfly.

Emperor Wang's passion was transformed into a calling cuckoo.

On a vast sea, when the moon is bright, pearls contain tears.

At Indigo Field, when the sun is warm, jade engenders smoke.

This passion might have become a memory to stop time

but is at this instant already dispossessed.

LI SHANGYIN

Untitled (I)

The chance to meet is difficult,

       but parting is even more difficult.

The east wind is powerless

       as the hundred flowers wither.

A spring silkworm spins silk

       up to the instant of death.

A candle only stops weeping

       when its wick becomes ash.

In the morning mirror, she grieves

       that the hair on her temples whitens.

Chanting poems in the evening,

       she only senses the moonlight's cold.

From here, Peng Mountain is not too far.

       O Green Bird, seek, seek her out.

Untitled (II)

Phoenix tails, fragrant silk,
        so many thin folds.
Under the round green canopy,
        she opens herself to the night.
A fan cuts the moon's shape
        but can't conceal her blush.
The carriage goes, thunder sounds;
        the words couldn't get through.
A while in the deep quiet,
        gold embers scintillate:
nothing now but the ebb and flow of
        pulsing red pomegranate wine.
A piebald horse is yet tied
        to a dangling willow.
And where out of the southwest
        can the fine breeze blow?

The Leyou Tombs

Toward evening,
      I was uneasy and restless.
I urged my carriage
      up to an ancient mound.
The setting sun
      was boundlessly beautiful,
but it was
      near the yellow dusk.

LI SHANGYIN

On a Rainy Night, Lines to Be Sent North

You ask me when I return, but I know not when.
The pools here at Ba Shan overflow with rain.
When will we trim candles by the western window
and the rain of this evening be in our words?

LI YU

To the Tune of "Meeting Happiness"

Silent and alone, I ascend the west tower.
The moon is like a hook.
In solitude, the *wutong* trees
imprison the clear autumn in the deep courtyard.
Scissored but not severed,
trimmed but still massive:
it is the sorrow of parting,
another strange flavor in the heart.

LI YU

To the Tune of "Joy in the Oriole's Flight"

The dawn moon begins to sink,
and last night's mist dissolves.
Speechless, I toss on my pillow:
my dream is of a return to fragrant grasses
and my thoughts cling, cling to them.
In the distant sky, the geese call once and are gone.

The orioles cry, then scatter,
leaving the last of the blossoms to decay.
I'm terribly alone in the deep court:
do not let the last of the red petals be swept away
but leave them for the dancing girls
to step on as they walk home.

SU DONGPO

Spring Night

Spring night: one-quarter of an hour
is worth a thousand pieces of gold.

Flowers have clear fragrance;
the moon has shadow.

Songs and flutes on the upstairs terrace;
the threadlike sound is fine, fine.

A rope-swing in the still courtyard,
where night is deep, deep.

LI QINGZHAO

To the Tune of "Intoxicated in the Shadows of Flowers"

Thin mist, dense clouds, a grief-stricken day;
auspicious incense burns in the gold animal.
Once again, it is the joyous mid-autumn festival,
but a midnight chill
touches my jade pillow and silk bed-screen.

I drink wine by the eastern fence in the yellow dusk.
Now a dark fragrance fills
my sleeves and makes me spin.
The bamboo blinds sway in the west wind.
And I am even thinner than a yellow flower.

To the Tune of "Telling My Most Intimate Feelings"

When night comes,
        I am so flushed with wine,
I undo my hair slowly:
        a plum calyx is
                stuck on a damaged branch.
I wake dazed when smoke
            breaks my spring sleep.
The dream distant,
        so very distant;
                and it is quiet, so very quiet.
The moon spins and spins.
The kingfisher blinds are drawn;
        and yet I rub the injured bud,
            and yet I twist in my fingers this fragrance,
            and yet I possess these moments of time!

MA ZHIYUAN

To the Tune of "Plum Blossoms in the Breeze": Evening Bell at a Misty Temple

Thin cold smoke,
> old still temple.
Near yellow dusk,
> and all the worshippers gone.
A soft west wind
> sounds the bell three, four times.

How can the old master
> practice *dhyana*?

MA ZHIYUAN

To the Tune of "Sailing at Night" (I)

When all hope of
        profit and fame is gone,
yes and no, right and wrong
        lose their meanings.
The world no longer
        draws me to the front door.
Green trees lean over
        and shade a corner of the house.
Blue hills fill to perfection
        the space over the wall.
Here is a simple
        bamboo fence and thatched cottage.

MA ZHIYUAN

To the Tune of "Sailing at Night" (II)

Think of the Qin palace
　　　　　and Han imperial city.
It is all wilds now
　　　　　where oxen and sheep graze.
If it were not like this,
　　　　　fishermen and woodcutters would have nothing to say.
North and south, tombs in the wilds.
　　　　　East and west, gravestones smashed.
Lying-Dragon and Leaping-Horse
　　　　　were once famous generals.
Now it is impossible to distinguish
　　　　　dragon from snake on the stones.

MA ZHIYUAN

To the Tune of "Sky-Clear Sand": Autumn Thoughts

Withered vine,
old tree,
crows.

A small bridge,
flowing water,
houses.

Ancient road,
west wind,
lean horse.

Sun sinking
in the west—

and a man,
crushed,
at the sky's edge.

SHEN ZHOU

Inscribed on a Painting

White clouds, like a sash,
                wind around the mountain's waist.
Stone steps rise into the void
                on this steep narrow path.
Alone, leaning on a chenopod staff,
                I gaze into the expanse
and wish to respond to the murmuring mountain stream
                by playing my bamboo flute.

BADA SHANREN

Globefish

from the third of four album leaves,
where a poem accompanies each painting

A fine rain drizzles and drizzles
on Yellow Bamboo Village.
A light boat bobs and bobs
among waves and clouds.
How can you get
a meal of yellow sprouts?
In May, globefish
are swallowed upside down.

BADA SHANREN

Bamboo

from the last of four album leaves

I sketch bamboo with cinnabar,
yet the cinnabar does not do it.
Just now, above the waters of the Xiang,
dragonflies, and rosy clouds.

BADA SHANREN

From a Painting of a Cat

Nanquan wanted to be reborn as a water buffalo,
but who did the body of the malicious cat become?
Black clouds and covering snow are alike.
It took thirty years for clouds to disperse, snow to melt.

BADA SHANREN

Inscription for a Painting

Summer solstice: on Zhang Tai Street,
I dab a corpselike cloud image with a brush.
Of the chronicles recited on the ancient terrace,
where is the wind that will wash them away?

Bright Light and Cloud Shadows

from the first of ten album leaves

Spring mountains have no near or far.
A thought of the past instantly becomes a forest.
With no place where clouds are not flying,
how did a worldly thought come to mind?

WANG YUYANG

Smelting Spring

The Red Bridge flies across the water—
in a single flow, the railing's nine red curves.
Noon: a painted boat passes under the bridge:
the clothes' fragrance, people's shadows, fleeting, fleeting.

Dead Water

Here is a ditch of hopelessly dead water.
A cool breeze would not raise the slightest ripple on it.
You might throw in some scraps of copper and rusty tins,
or dump in as well the remains of your meal.

Perhaps the green on copper will turn into emeralds,
or the rust on tin will sprout a few peach blossoms.
Let grease weave a layer of fine silk-gauze, and
mold steam out a few red-glowing clouds.

Let the dead water ferment into a ditch of green wine,
floating with pearls of white foam;
but the laughter of small pearls turning into large pearls
is broken by spotted mosquitoes stealing the wine.

Thus a ditch of hopelessly dead water
can yet claim a bit of something bright.
And if the frogs can't endure the utter solitude,
let the dead water burst into song.

Here is a ditch of hopelessly dead water.
Here beauty can never reside.
You might as well let ugliness come and cultivate it,
and see what kind of world comes out.

Perhaps

Perhaps you have wept and wept, and can weep no more.
Perhaps. Perhaps you ought to sleep a bit;
then don't let the nighthawk cough, the frogs
croak, or the bats fly.

Don't let the sunlight open the curtain onto your eyes.
Don't let a cool breeze brush your eyebrows.
Ah, no one will be able to startle you awake:
I will open an umbrella of dark pines to shelter your sleep.

Perhaps you hear earthworms digging in the mud,
or listen to the root hairs of small grasses sucking up water.
Perhaps this music you are listening to is lovelier
than the swearing and cursing noises of men.

Then close your eyelids, and shut them tight.
I will let you sleep; I will let you sleep.
I will cover you lightly, lightly with yellow earth.
I will slowly, slowly let the ashes of paper money fly.

Miracle

I never wanted the red of fire, the black at midnight
of the Peach Blossom Pool, the mournful melody of the *pipa,*

or the fragrance of roses. I never loved the stern
pride of the leopard, and no white dove ever had

the beauty I craved. I never wanted any of these things,
but their *crystallization*—a miracle ten thousand

times more rare than them all! But I am famished and harried.
I cannot go without nourishment: even if it is

dregs and chaff, I still have to beg for it. Heaven knows
I do not wish to be like this. I am by no means

so stubborn or stupid. I am simply tired of waiting,
tired of waiting for the miracle to arrive; and

I dare not starve. Ah, who doesn't know of how little worth
is a tree full of singing cicadas, a jug of turbid wine,

or smoky mountain peaks, bright ravines, stars
glittering in the empty sky? It is all so ordinary,

so inexorably dull, and it isn't worth our ecstatic joy,
our crying out the most moving names, or the

longing to cast gold letters and put them in a song.
I also affirm that to let tears come

at the song of an oriole is trivial, ridiculous,
and a waste of time. But who knows? I cannot be otherwise.

I am so famished and harried I take lamb's-quarters
and wild hyssop for fine grain—

                                    but there's no harm
in speaking clearly as long as the miracle appears.

Then at once I will cast off the ordinary. I will never
again gaze at a frosted leaf and dream of a spring blossom's

dazzle. I will not waste my strength, peel open
stones, and demand the warmth of white jade.

Give me one miracle, and I will never again whip ugliness,
and compel it to give up the meaning of its

opposite. Actually, I am weary of all this,
and these strained implications are hard to explain.

All I want is one clear word flashing like a Buddhist relic
with fierce light. I want it whole, complete,

shining in full face. I am by no means so stubborn
or stupid; but I cannot see a round fan without

seeing behind it an immortal face. So,
I will wait as many incarnations as it takes—

since I've made a vow. I don't know how many
incarnations have already passed; but I'll wait

and wait, quietly, for the miracle to arrive.
That day must come! Let lightning strike me,

volcanoes destroy me. Let all hell rise up and crush me!
Am I terrified? No, no wind will blow out

the light in me. I only wish my cast-off body
would turn into ashes. And so what? That, that minutest

fraction of time is a minutest fraction of—
ah, an extraordinary gust, a divine and stellar hush

(sun, moon, and spin of all stars stopped;
time stopped, too)—the most perfectly round peace.

I hear the sound of the door pivoting: and with it
the rustling of a skirt. That is a miracle.

And in the space of a half-open gold door,
you are crowned with a circle of light!

WEN YIDUO

The Last Day

Water sobs and sobs in the bamboo pipe gutter.
Green tongues of banana leaves lick at the windowpanes.
The four surrounding whitewashed walls are receding,
and I alone cannot fill such a large room.

A fire in a bowl burns and burns in my heart.
Silent, I wait for the faraway guest to arrive.
I feed the fire cobwebs, rat droppings,
and also the scaly skins of spotted snakes.

Now the crowing of a cock hastens a heap of ashes.
A gust of dark wind gropes at my mouth.
Ah, the guest is right in front of me!
I close my eyelids then follow him out.

YAN ZHEN

Good Harvest

Last winter,
the agricultural co-op was formed.
Two lovers sowed in this patch of land.
Seeds were sown into the mud.
Love was cultivated in the heart.

This spring,
a delicate rain sprinkles the land.
The tender buds flourish.
The two lovers, shoulder by shoulder,
come to weed.
Now they gaze into each other's eyes,
now bend down, smiling.

The summer has come.
The grains are ripe.
The date of marriage is set.
Who is not envious?
On the land of the co-op
is a harvest of bliss and love.

YAN ZHEN

The Plum Hint

Plums have bloomed, comrades.
Plum blossoms beckon you to come.
The productive team-captain plucks a branch,
and smiles as he walks into the village.

The snow on thousands of hills melted in one night.
A spout of water turns greener than before.
Listen! The cuckoo in the tree
also changes to a new tune.

Outside the village, ponds are full,
ditches dug, and millets green.
Inside the village the cows are fat,
horses strong, and carts adorned.
Who is trying the new whip?
The snapping is so strong!

The windows are open in every house.
In every mansion the doors are wide.
Oh, spring has come!
without signs or signals in advance.

Plums have bloomed, comrades.

The plum gardens crimson like clouds.

O you thousands of full-blooming plums

are like the ten thousand hearts of our commune members.

YAN ZHEN

On the Willow Bank

The riverbank is white like silver.
The morning moon, shaped like
a gold sickle, is standing on the snow.
The willows on both shores
are cast against thousands of clouds.
The traveling bells ring quick—
like beans jumping in the frying pan.

Bells ring quick, bells ring near;
the wheels speed on ahead.
The Red Banners sway in the wind
like peach blossoms in the groves.
The commune's cart is returning;
the snow whirls up to the sky.

O full-laden carts, what do you carry?
Seeds, tools, or fertilizers?
Passersby cannot see well
and stop on the road, asking.

The easing driver
brushes his hands and shrugs—

in a low voice,
"What we carry is spring."

Smiles the one who asks.
Smiles the one who answers.
Their smiles beam like the flashing wheels.
Wheels have trodden a thousand miles
and ahead will keep on flying.

YAN ZHEN

Red Rain

February rain, red rain,
is silently sprinkled on the South Yangtze.
A droplet tints a bone.
A droplet tints a smiling face.

Waters sound "splash splash" outside the village,
and a light rain smoke veils the villagestead.
Children running barefoot—
heads uplifted—run to welcome the drops of rain.

Young men gather round the commune gate
and finger the blade of the brand-new plow.
Everyone tries to plow the first furrow,
and all forget to wear their palm ponchos.

The tractor driver,
again and again, tries his new combine.
He continues to gaze at the unceasing rain,
which dances in circles in front of the windows.

A droplet tints a bone.
A droplet tints a smiling face.
February rain, red rain,
is silently spread on the South Yangtze.

YANG MU

The Star Is the Only Guide (I)

In the zone of rain shadows, at the moment of losing
my winding way, the star is the only guide
Your contemplation is an ocean, you are endless brooding
At night, in the morning, at the moment when mountain shadows
recede from my side table, we recall the time before exile

For the second time, you take off softly from
my backward gaze. Oh Lord—with the first posted mail
she stood amid blown-about rotting leaves
that night, in the downpour of lost love
Loneliness and morning bell chimes set you ablaze
It was me with a downward gaze
In my youthful gallop, you were the wind full in my face

(Yeh and Sze)

YANG MU

Water's Edge

I've been sitting here four afternoons
Not a single soul passes by—not to mention any sound of footsteps

(In loneliness—)

Spider brake grows from the crotch of my pants up to my shoulder
covering me for no reason
The cascade of flowing water is an indelible memory
All I can do is let it be scripted on a stilled cloud

Twenty meters to the south, a dandelion giggles
The pollen of the wind-pollinated flower lodges onto my bamboo hat
What can my hat offer you, come on
What can my shadow, lying down, offer you

Compare four afternoons of the water's sound to four afternoons
    of footsteps
Suppose they were some impatient teenage girls
bickering endlessly among themselves—
Well then, let none of them come. All I want is an afternoon nap
Well, let none of them come

(Yeh and Sze)

CHEN LI

Little Deaths

from Jiří Kylián's dance Petite Mort

Under the wind's quilt, each day
little deaths

Under the quilt's waves, you and I
brandish a sword of nothingness

A sword stabs into the body
to kill you, kill me

A sword stabs into the heart
to kill time, to utterly kill time

Where the tip of the sword points, little
orgasms belong to the quilt

Where the flashing sword passes, little
triumphant shouts and sobs

Little deaths make us
gradually accustomed to the humble triviality of living

Little conquests and surrenders
where neither enemy nor allied troops are on time's plain

Killers and instigators to the other
Assassins and pilgrims to the other

In the lifelong, indolent process of living,
process of dying, indolently

Inverting the sword handle into a pendulum, each day
little vibrations, little deaths

CHEN LI

Tango for the Jealous

If you embrace love as if it were a dishwasher,
ignore the greasy scars left on the dishes
licked by others' tongues or slashed by
the lengths of their knives and forks. Start the cycle
and flush them: forgetting is the best detergent.
Remember only the glorious, beautiful, shining parts,
because platters, especially china, are delicate.
Wash them, dry them, and, like a brand-new man,
greet tomorrow's breakfast as if nothing has happened.

Especially when your life is approaching or has passed
noon, youthful anxiety comes back to you again.
You pick up the phone and dial her in vain.
Suspicious and fretful, you make even more mute
and aimless phone calls to your invisible rivals in love.
You call that one again and again (oh how convenient,
modern communication), only to be answered
by an afternoon empty as a big bowl. Now, please
unplug the dishwasher for the moment, and swallow
the tangled phone wires like a mass of noodles,
splashed with a little of enmity's soy sauce.
The dishwasher will quickly rinse off your disgrace.

However, the dark night is an even bigger dishwasher,
when you're aggrieved and all the past dishes are flung at you—
unwashable bits of starlight stuck to the dish bottoms.
Ah, ignore the noise of the machine in operation,
the hum of the dark universe that won't go away.
Ignore the shadows that encircle you like leftover
fish bones, if the one you love is not by your side.
If you still feel like spitting out those irritating fish spines,
rearrange them, stroke after stroke, into new lines of poetry.

YAN LI

The Chinese Drawers

I pull out the Chinese drawers, one by one,
take a look at the years that I lived through.
In one drawer, those texts of
underground poems used to wrench themselves;
now, in the quiet, I can hear
the sounds of their retirement.

In another drawer
are a few grain coupons which are already antiques;
from the day they became obsolete,
I knew, even though they were cultural treasures,
they never took pride
in these crops from this land.

In another drawer
are two Red Guard bands,
one rusty 50 percent steel watch,
and a couple of photos from the April 5, 1976,
memorial in Tiananmen Square—
they all have the somber quiet after sacrifice.

The drawers, the Chinese drawers:
even pulling them out
from the bodies of the *five evil breeds*—
a Red Book must be in there.

YANG LIAN

Island (#2)

You're right   in life's chamber music
either listen with total attention   or else switch off
Water   one drop can perfectly lock up these shores

The crash of waves has no gap   is like a tailored body
still sitting on the rock   the lilac-scented surrounding ocean
still striking at a little girl's unceasing gaze into distance

Purple or white   petals are stored in the eyes
all through the springtime night, dark rings around the eyes
keep opening   torn by where she looks far away

Suffering is that waiting, underwater pearl
What turns old is salt   low sobbing in every wave
The fierce wind is a jade bracelet on the wrist

Island   like a boat sailing since the day you were born
never slowing down its disconsolate speed
always arriving yet, underfoot, drawn away by the ebbing tide

Purple   wounds the turbulent, close-up scene
sets off white   the horizon like land cutting, above snowline, into fate
exposing the snow flower you've caught for life

Still wet   tears run halfway down the girl's cheeks
After so many years   play the cold rain you've brought back
A seagull plunges   then flies back up   You hear clearly this kiss

YANG LIAN

Memorial to a Tree at the Street Corner

last night   my poem moved to the street corner
enacted a tree   waved
small white flowers that suddenly turned their faces like ghosts

screaming on tiptoe   permeated the air
ankle bones sparkled like crystals
the Tang dynasty like a lantern suddenly switched on

already it's been so many years   along a redbrick wall
I turned a corner it was the old country   at branch tip
familiar bloodshed finds again its stand-in

throws out tons of quicksilver colors
but I am no longer scared of shriveling   since a spring night
washed away   at the tree stump the lingering sound of an electric saw

WANG XIAONI

Very White Moonlight

The moon in the deep night lights every sliver of bone.

I inhale blue-white air.
The world's trifles and smatterings
turn into sinking fireflies.
The city's a carcass.

No living thing
matches this pure nighttime color.
At the window, I open curtains:
before my eyes, heaven and earth merge in argentine white.
In moonlight, I forget I'm a human being.

The last scene of life
is quietly rehearsed in a shadow of plain color.
Moonlight reaches the floorboards:
my two feet have already whitened beforehand.

ZHAI YONGMING

The Loneliness of Fireworks

Fireworks and bar girls
all dance in revelry
before they subside in the end into loneliness.

Moralists may not agree
at how naturally they explode in heaven—
we look as we please, consider as we please—
while the overlooked corners are suddenly illuminated.

If I, also, could be lifted into the sky,
I'd wish to be blown apart;
for love, I'd dance and shoot straight up.
Anyone can go wild in this moonlight,
when the moon's drenched in its own bliss.

And, if it could,
the moon itself would detonate
and, in every direction,
        spray out its entire body of flowery bones.

WANG JIAXIN

In Your Room

In your room, whatever you hang on your wall—
an image of a horse, a picture of the masters,
or even a sketch of St. Petersburg—
will become your self-portrait.

And on the street you walk, whatever you look at,
whichever tree, or whatever kind of person
you encounter, you too are one of them . . .
you, then, have no basis to be self-righteous.

WANG JIAXIN

Ice Anglers

In the reservoir near my house, when winter comes,
you can see some ice anglers,
squatting there in old army overcoats.
From a distance, they look like crows scattered in the snow.
They crouch there as if time has stopped.
They go there just so fish can breathe, under a single ray of light—
the fish swim hesitantly up to the holes.
The ice anglers' ecstasy is to see living creatures
thrash their tails in pain on ice,
until blood seeps from their gills,
staining red the piles of chiseled ice . . .
These are the most frightening sights I can imagine—
I turned away from that embankment;
I tried to think it was just a chance encounter on my stroll.

WANG JIAXIN

Fish Belly Poem

Dr. Xia Kejun said today:
there's no poetry in hell, and heaven doesn't require it either.
Great literature can only come from purgatory.

Sure, I agree. Destroyed in hell,
like in a gulag or the Jiabiangou labor camp—
there's a crowd of hungry ghosts and idiots there.
But are we in Dante's purgatory now?
No, I'm reminded of Jonah's legend—
The prophet Jonah was thrown into the ocean,
and a large fish swallowed him.
We, too, are in the belly of a fish;
it is dirty, but it seems warmer than the ocean outside.
This fish belly has hurricanes, floods. (Sometimes,
it floods up to your chest, like when you are stuck in a subway car!)
There are eerie clouds as dense as fish scales.
Yet there's care in this fish belly, and they summon us
to get vaccinated in the middle of the night.
In the fish belly, we just can't find
a table on which to write our great literature.
Does literature matter? We just want to live.
Jonah's eyes were wide open, and he prayed
in the fish belly for three days and three nights.

And we don't know
who the master of this big fish is.
We don't know if we can make it to the very end
or if we'll be spit out by this giant fish.

XI CHUAN

After Wang Ximeng's Blue and Green Horizontal Landscape Scroll, *A Thousand Miles of Rivers and Mountains*

Green colors and blue colors flow together and form empty mountains. Some people are walking in them, but they're still empty mountains, as if the people walking there have no faces, but they are still people. No one should try to recognize themselves in these figures, or try to see the real mountains and waters of this world, nor should anyone think of trying to gain casual praise from Wang Ximeng. Wang Ximeng knows these small figures, and that not one is he himself. These are not his figures, and he cannot call out a single one by name. The figures acquire the mountains and waters, just as the mountains acquire the emerald and lapis, just as the waters acquire vastness and boats, just as Emperor Huizong singled out Wang Ximeng at eighteen years old, not knowing that Wang would die soon after he finished this thousand miles of rivers and mountains. The mountains and waters are nameless. Wang Ximeng realizes that people without names are just decorations in mountains and waters, just as flying birds know they are insignificant to men's games. And the birds meet in the sky. Meanwhile, people walking in the mountains have their own directions to travel and their own plans. These small figures, in white, walk, sit at leisure, go fishing, trade, surrounded by green colors and blue colors, just as today, people, in black, go to banquets, concerts, and funerals, surrounded by golden colors and more golden colors. These small figures in white have never been born and so have never died; just like Wang Ximeng's landscape utopia, they are immune to pollution and invasion, and that is worth careful consideration. So people who are far away from social controls have no need to long for freedom, and people who haven't been destroyed by experience aren't concerned about forgetting. Wang Ximeng let the fishermen have infinite numbers of fishes to go fishing; he allowed limitless waters to run out from the mountains. According to him, happiness means the exact amount of blessing so that, immersed in the silence between mountains and waters, people can build bridges, waterwheels, roads, houses, and live quietly, just like the trees growing appropriately in the mountains, along the margins of water, or surrounding a village, and surrounding people. In the distance, the trees are like flowers. When they sway, it's the time when the clear wind is rising. When the clear wind is rising, it's time for people to sing. When people sing, it's time for an empty mountain to become an empty mountain.

JIANG TAO

Air Force One

The airplane cuts through thick clouds, bringing forth the
   archipelago's anxiety
Crawling on the reef, those soldiers
on military maneuvers just learned to say "hello"
Now they have to suddenly stand up
in the Okinawan town hall ablaze with lights

while you, President in a black body,
great lover of one black body,
tonight, where are you going to stay?
In bed next door, which Secretary of State, in white body, is it
who illuminates Asian affairs?

Out of the Pacific undercurrent, who can
swim slowly toward here, appearing
in a round cap with a single star,
and, knocking for you, say,

"Buddy, it's still early,
let's go out for a walk"?

Notes to Poems

RETURN TO QIANG VILLAGE

li: a Chinese mile, about one-third of a Western mile.

NIGHT AT THE TOWER

Lying-Dragon and Leaping-Horse are epithets for Zhuke Liang and Gongsun Shu, two famous Han-dynasty generals.

FLYING LIGHT

The allusions in "Flying Light" are extremely difficult. In this poem, the speaker laments the brevity of life and wants to slay the dragon that draws the sun across the sky—to stop time and recover peace. He considers the use of elixirs (yellow gold, white jade) to become an immortal ineffectual and derides Liu Che (Emperor Wudi of the Han) and Ying Zheng (the First Emperor of Qin) for their attempts to build massive, grandiose tombs and immortalize themselves.

There is a story that Ying Zheng died on a journey; his followers, anxious to keep his death a secret, filled a carriage with rotting abalone to disguise the stench of his decomposing body, then smuggled his corpse back into the capital.

One commentary says that the Spirit Lady was worshipped by the Han emperor and that the Great Unity was the supreme deity of the Daoists. I think the speaker is searching for ultimate knowledge and believes the Spirit Lady has it.

The Ruo tree is a mythical tree in the far west, whose foliage is supposed to glow red at sunset. Intriguingly, Li He places the Ruo tree in the east.

Ren Hungzi appears to be an immortal; the emperors are "just a heap of bones," whereas Ren Hungzi, an utter unknown, has somehow achieved the transcendence that they sought.

SONG OF THE COLLATOR'S SWORD IN THE SPRING BUREAU

This is another challenging poem. I think it is essentially an ode to the sword and its power.

Li He's elder cousin was employed as a collator in the Spring Bureau, secretariat of the household of the Crown Prince. Jing Ge tried to assassinate the first emperor of Qin. Indigo Field was famous for its jade. Liu Bang, founder of the Han dynasty, killed a snake; that night in a dream, an old woman appeared, cried, and said that he had unwittingly killed her son, the White King of the West.

AUTUMN COMES

Li He despairs that his work will not be recognized in his lifetime: "Who will ever read the green bamboo slips of this book?" Yet he believes that his work may be uncovered a thousand years later and that his poems will be transformed into green jade.

Before the invention of paper, books were written on slips of bamboo that were bound together. Bao Zhao, a fifth-century poet, obsessed over mortality in his poem "Graveyard Lament." In the *Zhuangzi,* there's an anecdote about a man who was unjustly put to death: three years after his burial, his blood had miraculously turned into green jade.

THE BROCADE ZITHER

There are many commentaries on this famous poem by Li Shangyin. Presence and absence, dream and reality, the solid and the insubstantial: the poem uses these polarities to explore the memory of love. Behind the first line, there's a story that the musical instrument, the *chin se,* originally had fifty strings; but when the Zhou emperor listened to the music, he found it unbearably sad and ordered the instrument broken in half. In the third line, there's a reference to the *Zhuangzi:* Zhuangzi once dreamed he was a butterfly; when he woke up, he didn't know if he was Zhuangzi who dreamed he was a butterfly or a butterfly who dreamed he was Zhuangzi. In the fourth line, there's another story: Wangti, King of Shu, committed adultery and died of shame; after his death, his soul was transformed into the cuckoo.

Mount Lantian, Indigo Field, was famous for its jade; it is said that the sun creates amazing visions there. These visions, however, can only be seen from far away; up close, they dissolve like smoke.

UNTITLED (I)
In this veiled love poem, the first two lines reveal the situation, but then lines three and four show that the poet is as powerless to prevent the beauty of his beloved from passing as he is flowers from withering. In lines five and six, the famous phrase, "A spring silkworm spins silk / up to the instant of death," may be read as an image of a poet spinning poems up to the moment of death; it can also be read as an image of endless longing, and the phrases "silkworm" and "silk thread" contain homonyms for "love spasms" and "amorous thoughts." In lines nine and ten, the poet imagines his lover sitting alone in front of a mirror— she is near and yet so far away.

Peng Mountain is the legendary mountain in the Eastern Sea. The green bird is a messenger of the Queen Mother of the West. At the end of this poem, the speaker's longing reaches out to the infinite.

TO THE TUNE OF "MEETING HAPPINESS"
wutong trees: Mathews's *Chinese-English Dictionary* says, "A tree, *Sterculia platanifolia;* it is sometimes called the national tree of China; the trunk is straight and beautifully green; it is said to be the only tree on which the phoenix will rest."

EVENING BELL AT A MISTY TEMPLE
dhyana: in Buddhism, a fixed state of contemplation.

MIRACLE
pipa: a musical instrument, known as the balloon-guitar.

LITTLE DEATHS
Jiří Kylián is a Czech former dancer and contemporary dance choreographer.

The *five evil breeds* (landlords, counterrevolutionaries, richer-than-others farmers, bad people, right wingers) were groups of people castigated during the Cultural Revolution.

FISH BELLY POEM

Dr. Xia Kejun is a famous critic and professor at Renmin University in Beijing.

Jiabiangou is located on the edge of the desert in Jiuquan, Gansu province. It was a labor camp used to imprison intellectuals, former government officials, and dissidents. From 1957 to 1961, nearly 3,000 "rightists" were imprisoned there, and about 2,500 died of starvation.

The flooding refers to a torrential rain that swept through Zhengzhou, the provincial capital of Henan, on July 20, 2021. Water poured into Metro Line 5 and, in the flooded train, fourteen passengers died.

Biographical Notes

TAO YUANMING, TAO QIAN (365–427) was one of the great early poets. He was the first to celebrate the joys of drinking wine, and the illuminations that thereby came to him. He once worked as libationer for his district but soon resigned. He was then offered a job as keeper of records but also turned it down. Tao was always dissatisfied with official appointments and found, instead, contentment in his "fields and garden."

WANG HAN (687–726) passed the imperial examinations in 710 CE. Little else is known about him.

WANG WEI (701–761) was a great poet, painter, and musician. He is best known for his highly condensed and powerful *jueju* (quatrains). His late work, "The Wang River Sequence," has still not been fully appreciated for its remarkable combination of lyric, dramatic, and symbolic elements that form an interior journey.

LI BAI (701–762) was a free spirit who was once called "an immortal banished to earth." His poems reveal a strong Daoist influence and are remarkable for their lyric flow, spontaneity, and emotional power. According to legend, one night he leaned out of a boat to embrace the moon on the Yangtze River and fell in and drowned.

DU FU (712–770) wrote brilliant poems in the *lushi* (regulated verse) form. These poems are amazing for their incised language and tonal counterpoint. For many years he struggled without success to pass through the official examination system. He experienced imprisonment, exile, and dire poverty.

ZHANG JI (ca. 766–ca. 830) passed the imperial examinations and held various government posts. Little is known about his life.

BAI JUYI (772–846) is best known for such long poems as *Song of Unending Sorrow* and *Ballad of the Pipa*. His work has a lovely colloquial tone and has been extensively translated by Arthur Waley.

LIU ZONGYUAN (773–819) helped renovate classical Chinese prose. "Snow on the River" is a classic example of *ut pictura poesis*.

LI HE (790–816) wrote rich, complex poems that draw on Chinese shamanism and mythology. He was a child prodigy and, at age seven, stunned Han Yu when he wrote a poem for him, titled "A Tall Official Carriage Comes on a Visit." Each morning, Li He rode on horseback, dashed off rough phrases of poems and stuffed them in his saddlebag. Later in the day, he would lay out these phrases and incorporate them into poems.

DU MU (803–852) had a long career as a public official and served near the end of his life in the Grand Secretariat. His poems often express disillusionment and the yearning for a former golden era.

LI SHANGYIN (813–858) tried to pursue a career through the examination system but was blocked by numerous political rivalries and power struggles near the end of the Tang dynasty. His untitled poems are some of the great love poems in classical Chinese.

LI YU (937–978) wrote remarkable poems in the *ci* (lyric) genre. He was the last ruler of the Southern Tang; on his forty-first birthday, the Song emperor sent him a gift of poisoned wine.

SU SHI, SU DONGPO (1036–1101) was a distinguished calligrapher and painter as well as poet. He served as an administrator but fell into disfavor when he wrote the emperor a letter describing hardships his policies were causing. He was later imprisoned, released, and banished.

LI QINGZHAO (1084–1151) is generally considered to be China's finest woman poet. She was a master of the *ci* (lyric) genre and was a painter, calligrapher, and, along with her husband, an avid collector of and specialist in ancient stone and bronze inscriptions. Her happy years turned to tragedy, however, when in 1127 their house was destroyed by invading Tartars, and in 1129 her husband contracted typhoid fever and died.

MA ZHIYUAN (1260–1324) was an outstanding poet and playwright of the Yuan dynasty. Ma's *Autumn in the Palace of the Han* is a remarkable play that culminates in a moving depiction of the final autumnal desolation of an emperor. Ma also wrote many songs and song cycles. All the poems translated here are in the *qu* (song) form.

SHEN ZHOU (1427–1509) was a great painter, calligrapher, and poet of the Ming dynasty. He shunned an official career and instead lived at home taking care of his mother, who lived to be almost one hundred. He enjoyed fame as an artist and teacher.

ZHU DA, BADA SHANREN (1626–1705) was a descendant of the Ming imperial family but became a monk after the Manchu invasion led to the collapse of the Ming in 1644. In 1680, he became, or pretended to become, mad, mute, and given to fits of laughing and weeping. From about 1685 on, he signed all his paintings Bada Shanren, "Mountain Man of the Eight Greats." Chan Buddhism is a strong influence on his work. The poems translated here are all taken from his paintings.

WANG SHIZHEN, WANG YUYANG (1634–1711) was a native of Huantai, Shandong. He was a leading poet in the early Qing dynasty and frequently chose the Red Bridge in Yangzhou as the setting for literary and social gatherings.

WEN YIDUO (1899–1946) was a pivotal figure in early-twentieth-century Chinese poetry. He rejected classical Chinese, choosing to write in the vernacular, and yet his work shows a confluence of the two. He came to the United States, studying at the Art Institute of

Chicago and at Colorado College. When he returned to China, he became involved in the political turmoil of his time. On July 15, 1946, Wen gave an impassioned speech denouncing the Guomindang government and was assassinated later that day.

YAN ZHEN (twentieth century) published the poems I have translated in a Sichuan party newspaper in the late 1950s. Although these poems have terminology such as "comrades," they harken all the way back to the very first anthology of Chinese poetry, the *Shijing* (*The Book of Songs*).

YANG MU (1940–2020) was born in Hualien, Taiwan. He attended the Iowa Writers' Workshop and received an MFA from the University of Iowa in 1966 and then received a PhD in comparative literature from the University of California at Berkeley. For many years, he was a professor of comparative literature at the University of Washington and later became dean of the College of Humanities and Social Sciences at National Dong Hwa University, Taiwan. He was one of Taiwan's leading poets and published *Hawk of the Mind: Collected Poems of Yang Mu,* edited by Michelle Yeh (Columbia University Press, 2018).

CHEN LI (b. 1954) was born and raised in Hualien, Taiwan. He started writing poetry in the 1970s under the influence of modernism. He turned to social and political themes in the 1980s and, from the 1990s onward, has explored a wide range of subjects and styles, combining formal and linguistic experiments with concern for indigenous culture and the formation of a new Taiwanese identity. Winner of the National Award for Literature and Arts in Taiwan, he has published more than a dozen books of poetry. Chen Li is also a prolific prose writer and translator.

YAN LI (b. 1954) was born in Beijing and is a poet, editor, fiction writer, and painter. In 1985, he moved from Beijing to New York City and, in 1987, founded *First Line,* a quarterly journal that featured the works of contemporary Chinese poetry as well as American poetry in

Chinese translation. He is the author of six books of poetry and two novels, and was a member of a group of artists known as the Stars. More recently, he has moved back and forth between Shanghai and New York City.

YANG LIAN (b. 1955) was born in Switzerland and grew up in Beijing. He began writing when he was sent to the countryside in the 1970s. Yang Lian's poems became influential inside and outside of China in the 1980s, especially when his poem "Norlang" was criticized by the Chinese government during the "Anti-Pollution" movement. He became a poet in exile and has continued to write and speak out as a highly individual voice in world literature, politics, and culture. He was awarded the Flaiano International Poetry Prize (Italy, 1999), and his three volumes of collected works were eventually published in China. His many translations into English include *Yi,* a book-length poem (Green Integer, 2002) and *Anniversary Snow* (Shearsman Books, UK, 2019). He currently lives in Berlin.

WANG XIAONI (b. 1955) was born in Changchun, Jilin, and worked as a laborer for seven years during the Cultural Revolution. She graduated from Jilin University in 1982 and has worked as a film script editor and also taught at Hainan University. She has published more than twenty-five books of poetry, essays, and fiction. Her work in English is available in *Something Crosses My Mind,* translated by Eleanor Goodman (Zephyr Press & The Chinese University of Hong Kong Press, 2014). She lives in Shenzhen.

ZHAI YONGMING (b. 1955) was born in Chengdu and studied at the University of Electronic Science and Technology of China, earning her degree in 1981. Several years later, she rose to prominence with the publication of her twenty-poem cycle "Woman," a work that articulated a female point of view in China's largely patriarchal society. From 1990 to 1992, Zhai lived in the United States. In addition to being a poet, she is also a prolific essayist and installation artist. She owns a bar in Chengdu, where she hosts poetry readings and other cultural events. Her selected poems in English is *The Changing Room,* translated by Andrea Lingenfelter (Zephyr Press & The Chinese University of Hong Kong Press, 2011).

WANG JIAXIN (b. 1957) is a poet, translator, essayist, and critic. He was born in Hubei province and studied literature at Wuhan University. In the early 1990s, as a writer he traveled to England, the Netherlands, Belgium, and Germany. He is the author of seven books of poetry and ten books of critical essays, and is the leading translator of Paul Celan. He was a professor at Renmin University in Beijing and, at the invitation of the Dutch Foundation for Literature, was recently a writer in residence in Amsterdam. He has won a variety of domestic and foreign poetry awards, including the first Ai Qing Poetry Award (2023), and has published *Darkening Mirror: New and Selected Poems,* translated by Diana Shi and George O'Connell (Tebot Bach, 2016).

XI CHUAN (b. 1963) is a poet, essayist, and translator. He was born in Xuzhou, Jiangsu province. From 1981 to 1985, he received his education in the English department at Beijing University. For many years he taught classical and modern Chinese literature at the Central Academy of Fine Arts, and he is now a professor at the International Writing Center at Beijing Normal University. He has received many awards for his poetry, including the Lu Xun Prize (China), the Cikada Prize (Sweden), and the Tokyo Poetry Prize (Japan). His translations into English include *Bloom and Other Poems,* translated by Lucas Klein (New Directions, 2022).

JIANG TAO (b. 1970) is a poet and critic. He was born in Tianjin and studied biomedical engineering at Tsinghua University, then switched to literature. He received his PhD in Chinese literature from Beijing University and, as a professor, has taught at Beijing University since 2002. He has published four books of poetry and received the Liu Li'an Poetry Prize in 1997. He has recently published *For a Splendid Sunny Apocalypse,* translated by Josh Stenberg (Zephyr Press, 2023).

Acknowledgments

Grateful acknowledgment is made to the editors of the following publications in which these translations, sometimes in earlier versions, first appeared:

Asymptote: "The Star Is the Only Guide (I)" and "Water's Edge" by Yang Mu

The Bloomsbury Review: "Drinking Wine (I)" by Tao Qian

Bombay Gin: "Drinking Alone with the Moon" by Li Bai; "To the Tune of 'Meeting Happiness'" by Li Yu

Boston Review: "After Wang Ximeng's Blue and Green Horizontal Landscape Scroll, *A Thousand Miles of Rivers and Mountains*" by Xi Chuan

Buttons: "Return to Qiang Village" and "Spring View" by Du Fu

Columbia: "Moonlight Night" by Du Fu; "Easing My Heart" by Du Mu; "On the Willow Bank" by Yan Zhen

Denver Quarterly: "A Question Addressed to Mr. Liu" by Bai Juyi; "To the Tune of 'Joy in the Oriole's Flight'" by Li Yu; "Drinking Wine (III)" by Tao Qian

Faultline: "The Last Day" by Wen Yiduo

First Intensity: "The Brocade Zither," "The Leyou Tombs," "On a Rainy Night, Lines to Be Sent North," and "Untitled (I)" by Li Shangyin; "Bamboo Grove," "Deer Park," and "Xinyi Village" by Wang Wei

Gate (Germany): "The Lotus," "Night Thoughts," "Song of Zhanggan," and "To the Tune of 'Clear Happiness'" by Li Bai; "Highland" and "from 'Miscellaneous Poems'" by Wang Wei

Green Mountains Review: "Night at the Tower" by Du Fu; "Autumn Comes" by Li He

Gulf Coast: "Memorial to a Tree at the Street Corner" by Yang Lian

Hanging Loose: "Anchored at Qinhuai River" by Du Mu; "Sitting Alone with Jingting Mountain" by Li Bai; "Snow on the River" by Liu Zongyuan

The Kenyon Review: "Bright Light and Cloud Shadows," "Globefish," and "Inscription for a Painting" by Bada Shanren; "Untitled (II)" by Li Shangyin; "Inscribed on a Painting" by Shen Zhou; "Ice Anglers" by Wang Jiaxin

Kyoto Journal (Japan): "Xinyi Village" by Wang Wei; "Miracle" by Wen Yiduo

Luna: "Bamboo" and "From a Painting of a Cat" by Bada Shanren

Malini: "Dead Water" by Wen Yiduo

Malpaís Review: "Little Deaths" and "Tango for the Jealous" by Chen Li; "Night at the Tower" by Du Fu; "Drinking Alone with the Moon" by Li Bai; "To the Tune of 'Telling My Most Intimate Feelings'" by Li Qingzhao; "Evening Bell at a Misty Temple" by Ma Zhiyuan; "from 'Miscellaneous Poems'" by Wang Wei; "Dead Water" by Wen Yiduo; "After Wang Ximeng's Blue and Green Horizontal Landscape Scroll, *A Thousand Miles of Rivers and Mountains*" by Xi Chuan; "Island (#2)" and "Memorial to a Tree at the Street Corner" by Yang Lian; "The Chinese Drawers" by Yan Li

Mānoa: the introductory essay appeared under the title "Translating a Poem by Li Shang-yin"

Narrative: "from 'Miscellaneous Poems'" by Wang Wei; "The Loneliness of Fireworks" by Zhai Yongming

New Letters: "Song of the Collator's Sword in the Spring Bureau" by Li He

The New Mexican: "Drinking Wine (I)" by Tao Qian

Pax: "To the Tune of 'Intoxicated in the Shadows of Flowers'" by Li Qingzhao; "Drinking Wine (II)" and "Returning to Fields and Gardens" (I and II) by Tao Qian

Plume: "Fish Belly Poem" by Wang Jiaxin; "Smelting Spring" by Wang Yuyang

Poetry: "Island (#2)" by Yang Lian

Poetry International: "The Chinese Drawers" by Yan Li

The Portsmouth Review: "To the Tune of 'Telling My Most Intimate Feelings'" by Li Qingzhao; "Sending Off Mr. Yuan" by Wang Wei; "The Last Day" by Wen Yiduo

Puerto del Sol: "Question and Answer in the Green Mountains" by Li Bai; "Mooring at Night by the Maple Bridge" by Zhang Ji

The Santa Fe Reporter: "Autumn Thoughts" by Ma Zhiyuan

Shadowgraph: "Air Force One" by Jiang Tao

Sol Tide: "The Lotus" by Li Bai; "Good Harvest," "The Plum Hint," and "Red Rain" by Yan Zhen

Stooge: "Song of Liangzhou" by Wang Han

Tarasque: "Autumn Thoughts" and "Evening Bell at a Misty Temple" by Ma Zhiyuan; "Dead Water," "Miracle," and "Perhaps" by Wen Yiduo

2 Plus 2 (Switzerland): "Autumn Thoughts" and "To the Tune of 'Sailing at Night'" (I and II) by Ma Zhiyuan

Volt: "Flying Light" by Li He

Words Without Borders: "In Your Room" by Wang Jiaxin

The World: "Spring Night" by Su Dongpo

Zoland Poetry: "Little Deaths" and "Tango for the Jealous" by Chen Li

The Anchor Book of Chinese Poetry: From Ancient to Contemporary, the Full 3000-Year Tradition, edited by Tony Barnstone and Chou Ping

(Anchor, 2005): "Flying Light" by Li He; "Dead Water," "Miracle," and "Perhaps" by Wen Yiduo

Anthology of Magazine Verse & Yearbook of American Poetry, edited by Alan Pater (Monitor, 1985): "Drinking Wine (I)" by Tao Qian

A Century of Modern Chinese Poetry: An Anthology, edited by Michelle Yeh, Frank Stewart, and Zhangbin Li (University of Washington Press, 2023): "Little Deaths" and "Tango for the Jealous" by Chen Li; "Very White Moonlight" by Wang Xiaoni; "Dead Water" and "Perhaps" by Wen Yiduo; "Island (#2)" and "Memorial to a Tree at the Street Corner" by Yang Lian; "Water's Edge" by Yang Mu

The Ecco Anthology of International Poetry, edited by Ilya Kaminsky and Susan Harris (Ecco, 2010): "Perhaps" by Wen Yiduo; "After Wang Ximeng's Blue and Green Horizontal Landscape Scroll, *A Thousand Miles of Rivers and Mountains*" by Xi Chuan; "The Plum Hint" by Yan Zhen

Hawk of the Mind: Collected Poems of Yang Mu, edited by Michelle Yeh (Columbia University Press, 2018): "The Star Is the Only Guide (I)" and "Water's Edge" by Yang Mu

Into English: Poems, Translations, Commentaries, edited by Martha Collins and Kevin Prufer (Graywolf Press, 2017): "Returning to Fields and Gardens (I)" by Tao Qian

Lee Valley Poems by Yang Lian (Bloodaxe, UK, 2009): "Memorial to a Tree at the Street Corner" by Yang Lian

Literatures of Asia, Africa, and Latin America, edited by Tony Barnstone and Willis Barnstone (Prentice Hall, 1999): "Miracle" by Wen Yiduo

19 Ways of Looking at Wang Wei (with more ways), edited by Eliot Weinberger (New Directions, 2016): "Bamboo Grove" and "Deer Park" by Wang Wei

The Poem behind the Poem: Translating Asian Poetry, edited by Frank Stewart (Copper Canyon Press, 2004): "Return to Qiang Village" by

Du Fu; "Untitled (II)" by Li Shangyin; "Drinking Wine (I)" by Tao Qian; "The Last Day" and "Miracle" by Wen Yiduo

Poems for the Millenium, Volume One, edited by Jerome Rothenberg (University of California Press, 1995): "Dead Water" and "Miracle" by Wen Yiduo

The Third Shore: Chinese & English-Language Poets in Mutual Translation, edited by W.N. Herbert and Yang Lian (Shearsman Books, UK, 2013): "Air Force One" by Jiang Tao; "After Wang Ximeng's Blue and Green Horizontal Landscape Scroll, *A Thousand Miles of Rivers and Mountains*" by Xi Chuan; "The Chinese Drawers" by Yan Li

This Art: Poems about Poetry, edited by Michael Wiegers (Copper Canyon Press, 2003): "Thoughts on a Night Journey" by Du Fu

The Translator's Page, curated by Jonathan Wells (the Four Way Books website, 2022): "After Wang Ximeng's Blue and Green Horizontal Landscape Scroll, *A Thousand Miles of Rivers and Mountains*" by Xi Chuan; "Memorial to a Tree at the Street Corner" by Yang Lian

The Wadsworth Anthology of Poetry, edited by Jay Parini (Thomson Wadsworth, 2005): "Spring View" and "Thoughts on a Night Journey" by Du Fu; "Night Thoughts" and "Song of Zhanggan" by Li Bai; "Returning to Fields and Gardens" (I and II) by Tao Qian; "Song of Liangzhou" by Wang Han

The World Treasury of Poetry, edited by John Major and Kathleene Washburn (Norton, 1998): "Flying Light" by Li He; "Untitled (I)" by Li Shangyin; "To the Tune of 'Meeting Happiness'" by Li Yu; "Dead Water" by Wen Yiduo; "On the Willow Bank" by Yan Zhen

"Drinking Alone with the Moon" by Li Bai appeared as a broadside from Lumen Books.

"From a Painting of a Cat" by Bada Shanren appeared as a broadside from Copper Canyon Press.

Some of these translations also appeared in the second editions of *The Willow Wind* (Tooth of Time, 1981) and *Two Ravens* (Tooth of Time,

1984). Many of these translations appeared in *The Silk Dragon: Translations from the Chinese* (Copper Canyon Press, 2001).

I thank Steven Schwartz and the Witter Bynner Foundation for Poetry for two grants that gave me time and support to make many of these translations.

Thanks to Michael Wiegers, Ryo Yamaguchi, Marisa Vito, Claretta Holsey, and everyone at Copper Canyon Press for your support.

About the Translator

Arthur Sze is a poet, translator, and editor. He is the author of eleven books of poetry, including *The Glass Constellation: New and Collected Poems* (2021); *Sight Lines* (2019), for which he received the National Book Award; *Compass Rose* (2014), a Pulitzer Prize finalist; *The Ginkgo Light* (2009), selected for the PEN Southwest Book Award and the Mountains & Plains Independent Booksellers Association Book Award; *Quipu* (2005); *The Redshifting Web: Poems 1970–1998* (1998), selected for the Balcones Poetry Prize and the Asian American Literary Award; and *Archipelago* (1995), selected for an American Book Award. He has also published one previous book of Chinese poetry translations, *The Silk Dragon: Translations from the Chinese* (2001), selected for the Western States Book Award, and edited *Chinese Writers on Writing* (2010). A recipient of the Ruth Lilly Poetry Prize, the Shelley Memorial Award, the Jackson Poetry Prize, a Lannan Literary Award, a Guggenheim Fellowship, a Lila Wallace–Reader's Digest Writers' Award, two National Endowment for the Arts Creative Writing Fellowships, a Howard Foundation Fellowship, as well as five grants from the Witter Bynner Foundation for Poetry, Sze was the first poet laureate of Santa Fe, where he lives with his wife, the poet Carol Moldaw. From 2012 to 2017, he was a chancellor of the Academy of American Poets, and in 2017, he was elected a fellow of the American Academy of Arts and Sciences. His poems have been translated into fourteen languages, including Chinese, Dutch, German, Portuguese, and Spanish. He is a professor emeritus at the Institute of American Indian Arts.

Poetry is vital to language and living. Since 1972, Copper Canyon Press has published extraordinary poetry from around the world to engage the imaginations and intellects of readers, writers, booksellers, librarians, teachers, students, and donors.

WE ARE GRATEFUL FOR THE MAJOR SUPPORT PROVIDED BY:

academy of
american poets

OFFICE OF ARTS & CULTURE

SEATTLE

amazon *literary partnership*

THE PAUL G. ALLEN
FAMILY FOUNDATION

4
CULTURE

POETRY FOUNDATION

Hawthornden
Foundation

INGRAM
CONTENT GROUP

the **point**
envision · enact · evolve

Lannan

WASHINGTON STATE
ARTS COMMISSION

**National
Endowment
for the Arts**
arts.gov
ART WORKS.

The Witter Bynner Foundation
for Poetry

TO LEARN MORE ABOUT UNDERWRITING
COPPER CANYON PRESS TITLES,
PLEASE CALL 360-385-4925 EXT. 103

WE ARE GRATEFUL FOR THE MAJOR SUPPORT PROVIDED BY:

Anonymous

Richard Andrews and
    Colleen Chartier

Jill Baker and Jeffrey Bishop

Anne and Geoffrey Barker

Donna Bellew

Will Blythe

John Branch

Diana Broze

John R. Cahill

Sarah Cavanaugh

Keith Cowan and Linda Walsh

Stephanie Ellis-Smith and
    Douglas Smith

Mimi Gardner Gates

Gull Industries Inc.
    on behalf of William True

Carolyn and Robert Hedin

David and Jane Hibbard

Bruce S. Kahn

Phil Kovacevich and Eric Wechsler

Maureen Lee and Mark Busto

Ellie Mathews and Carl Youngmann
    as The North Press

Larry Mawby and Lois Bahle

Petunia Charitable Fund and
    adviser Elizabeth Hebert

Suzanne Rapp and Mark Hamilton

Adam and Lynn Rauch

Emily and Dan Raymond

Joseph C. Roberts

Cynthia Sears

Kim and Jeff Seely

Tree Swenson

Barbara and Charles Wright

In honor of C.D. Wright,
    from Forrest Gander

Caleb Young as C. Young Creative

The dedicated interns and faithful
    volunteers of Copper Canyon Press

The pressmark for Copper Canyon Press
suggests entrance, connection, and interaction
while holding at its center
an attentive, dynamic space for poetry.

This book is set in Monotype Bembo Book Pro.
Book design by Gopa & Ted2, Inc.
Printed on archival-quality paper.